BOOK 1

A vibrant collection of original pieces for piano

Un vibrant recueil de pièces originales pour piano

Eine reizvolle Sammlung von Origininalkompositionen für Klavier

Elissa Milne

© 2006 by Faber Music Ltd
First published in 2006 by Faber Music Ltd
Bloomsbury House
74–77 Great Russell Street
London WC1B 3DA
Cover illustration by Dave Wood
Music processed by Christopher Hinkins
Printed in England by Caligraving Ltd
All rights reserved

ISBN10: 0-571-52371-4
EAN13: 978-0-571-52371-9

To buy Faber Music publications or to find out about the full range of titles available
please contact your local music retailer or Faber Music sales enquiries:

Faber Music Limited, Burnt Mill, Elizabeth Way, Harlow, CM20 2HX England
Tel: +44 (0)1279 82 89 82   Fax: +44 (0)1279 82 89 83
sales@fabermusic.com   fabermusic.com

Run ragged

Elissa Milne

Clumsy cowboy

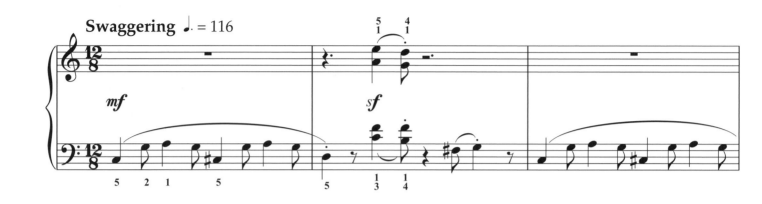

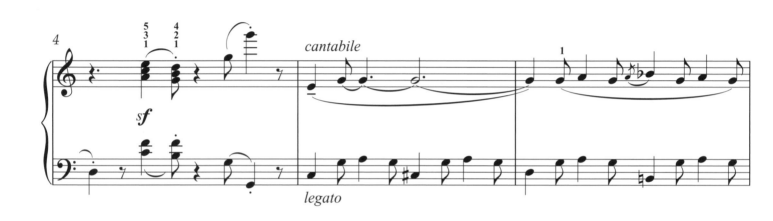

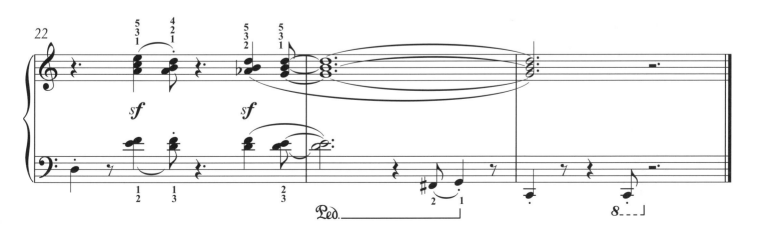

Scoot

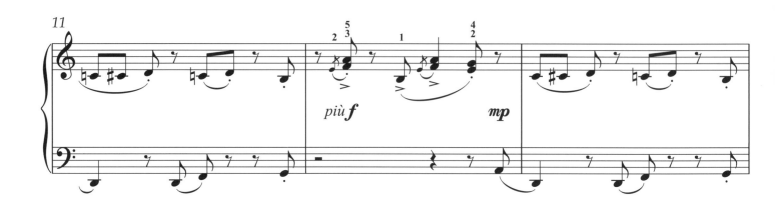

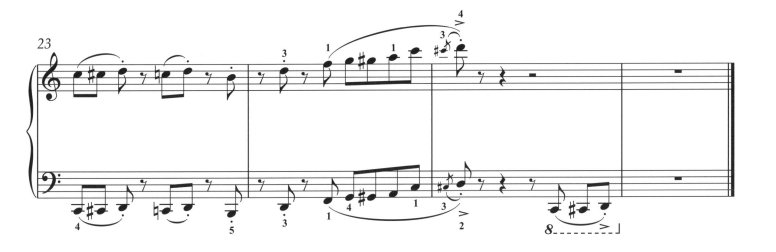

Where the wind blows

Tartan

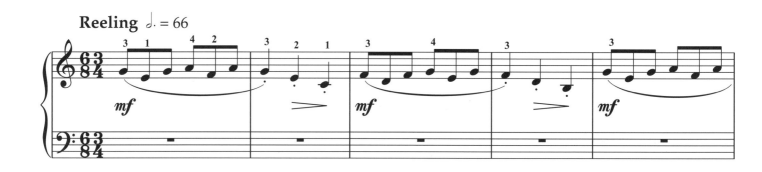

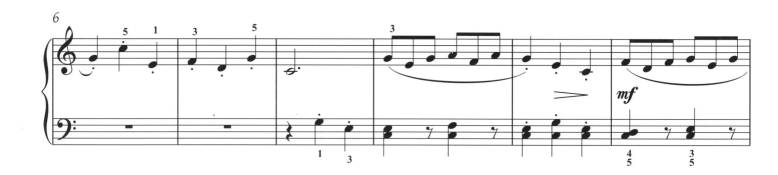

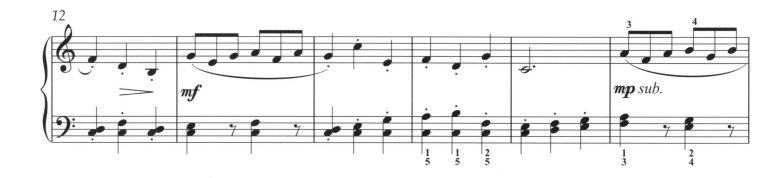

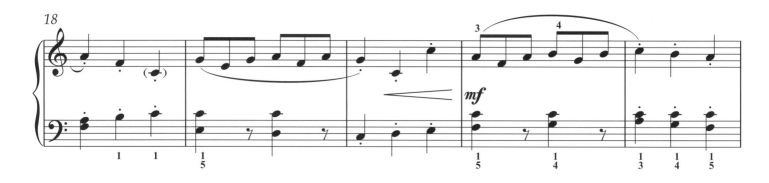

Antarctic breeze

In search of lost time

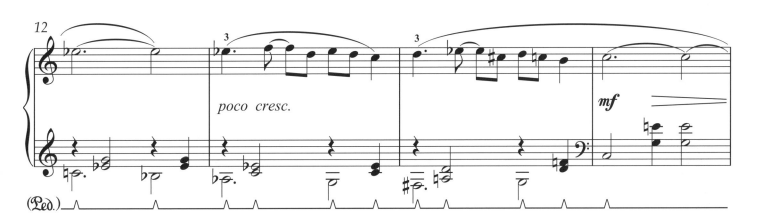

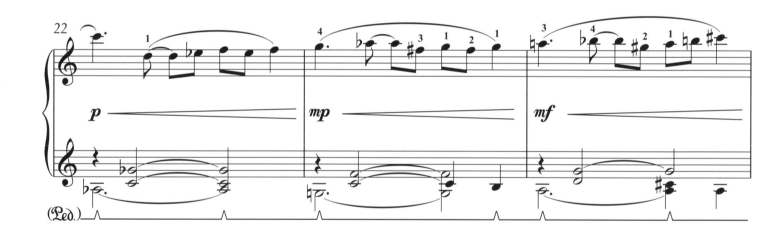

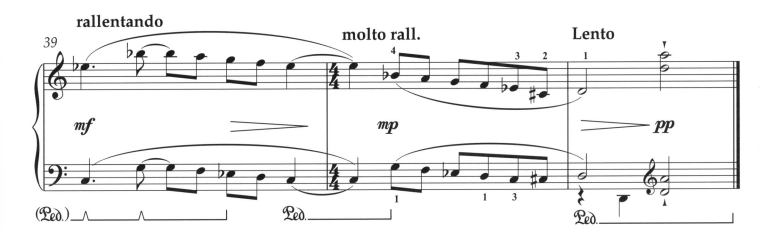

Daylight robbery

Drill

With precision (no faster than ♩ = 120)

Mischief

Stomp

Gone too soon

Mulga Bill

Mulga Bill is a character in a Banjo Patterson poem. Riding home on his
new bicycle, he comes to grief descending a steep slope to a shallow creek ...

Hurtling ♩ = 138

Mulga Bill

Mulga Bill is a character in a Banjo Patterson poem. Riding home on his
new bicycle, he comes to grief descending a steep slope to a shallow creek ...

Book 'em

Arrestingly ♩ = 126

Book 'em